Castles, Caves, and Honeycombs

LINDA ASHMAN

Illustrated by LAUREN STRINGER

SCHOLASTIC INC.
New York Toronto London Auckland Sydney
Mexico City New Delhi Hong Kong Buenos Aires

Special thanks to my editor, Allyn Johnston,
who knows when to gently push me back into shape
—L. S.

The illustrations in this book were painted in Lascaux acrylics on Fabriano 140 lb. watercolor paper.
The display type was set in Gasteur.
The text type was set in Throhand Ink.
Designed by Lydia D'moch and Lauren Stringer.

Text copyright © 2001 by Linda Ashman.
Illustrations copyright © 2001 by Lauren Stringer.
All rights reserved. Published by Scholastic Inc., 557 Broadway, New York, NY 10012,
by arrangement with Harcourt, Inc.
Printed in the U.S.A.

ISBN 0-439-85706-6

SCHOLASTIC and associated logos and designs are
trademarks and/or registered trademarks of Scholastic Inc.

2 3 4 5 6 7 8 9 10   40   14 13 12 11 10 09 08

To Jack and Jackson,
who make my home such a happy one
—L. A.

For my mom,
who made us a home wherever we went,
and for M., R., and C.
—L. S.

Many places make a home—
A heap of twigs.

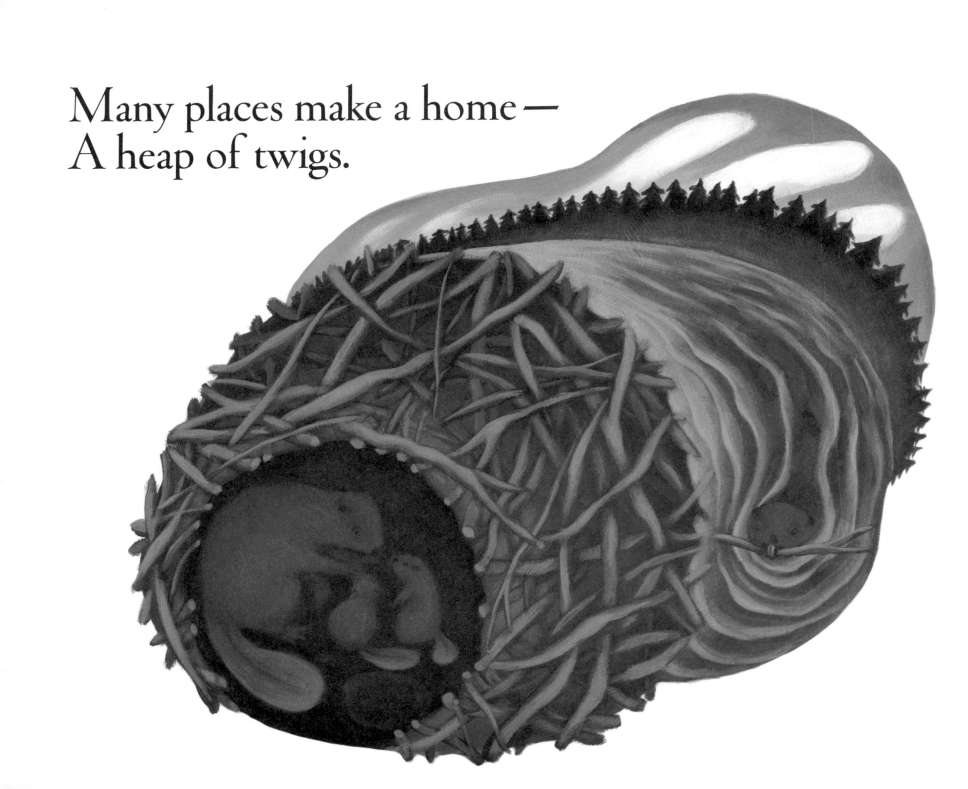

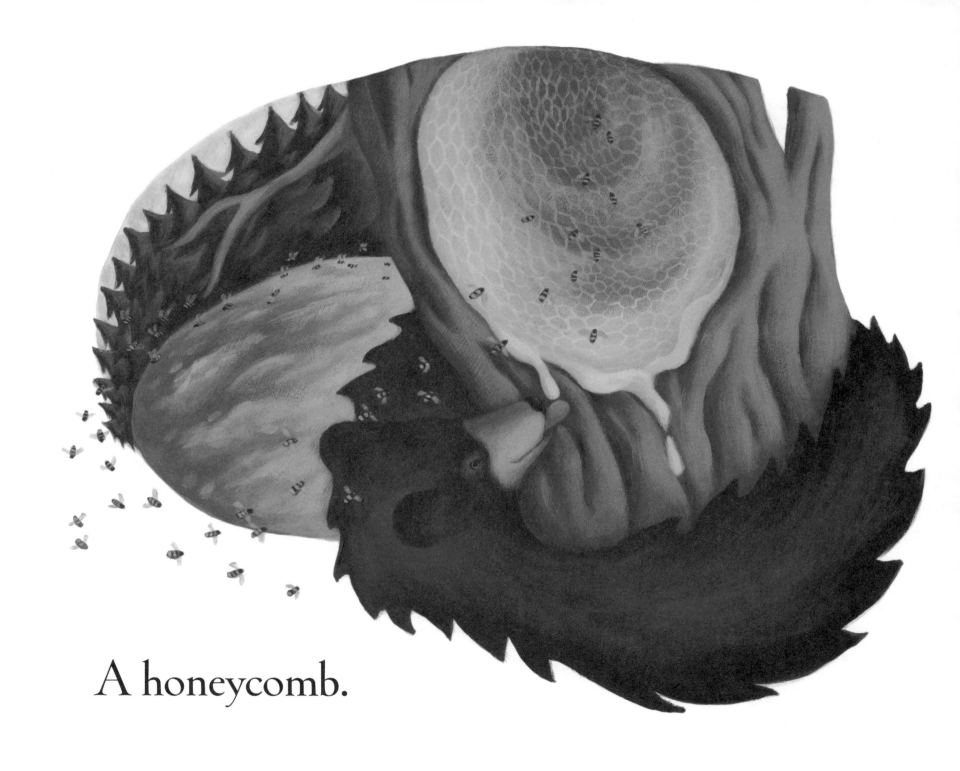

A honeycomb.

A castle with
a tower or two.

An aerie with
a bird's-eye view.

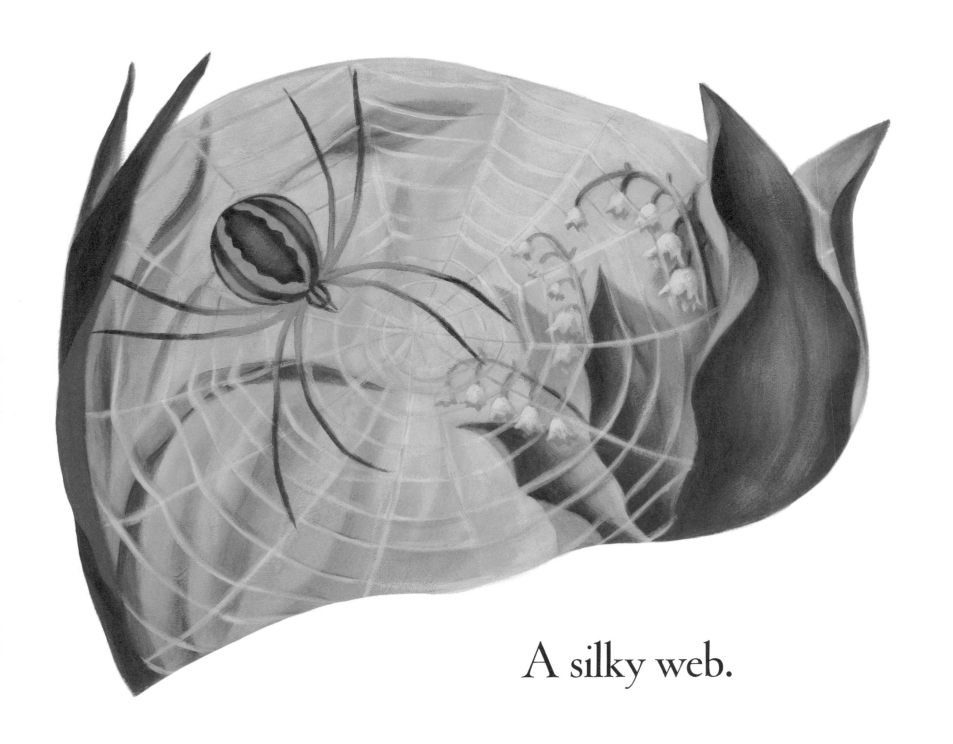

A silky web.

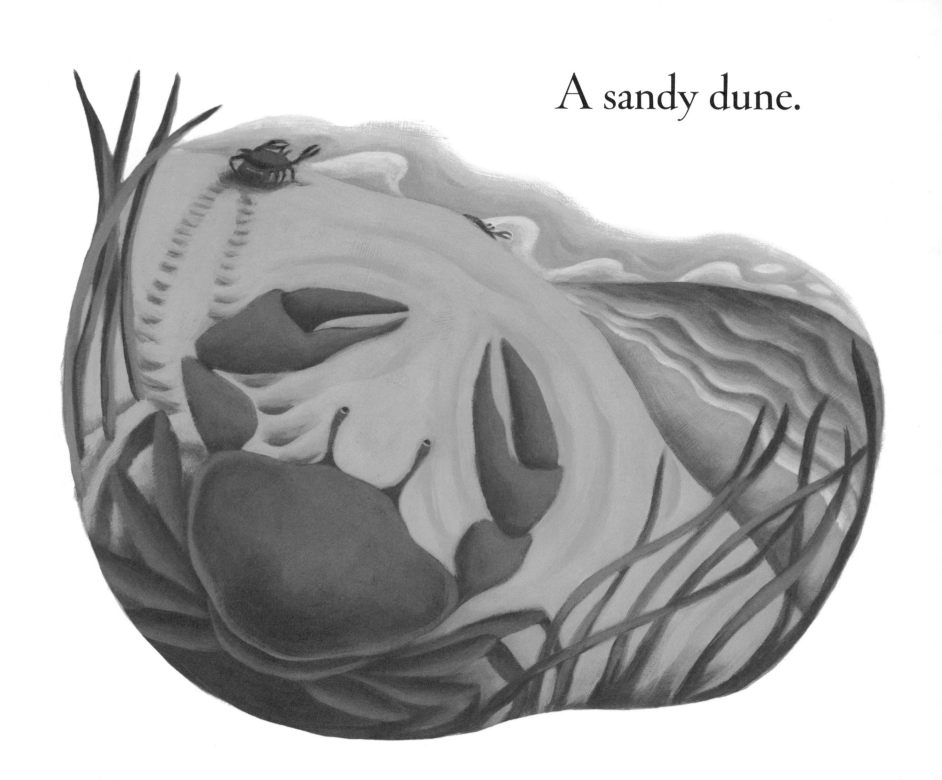

A sandy dune.

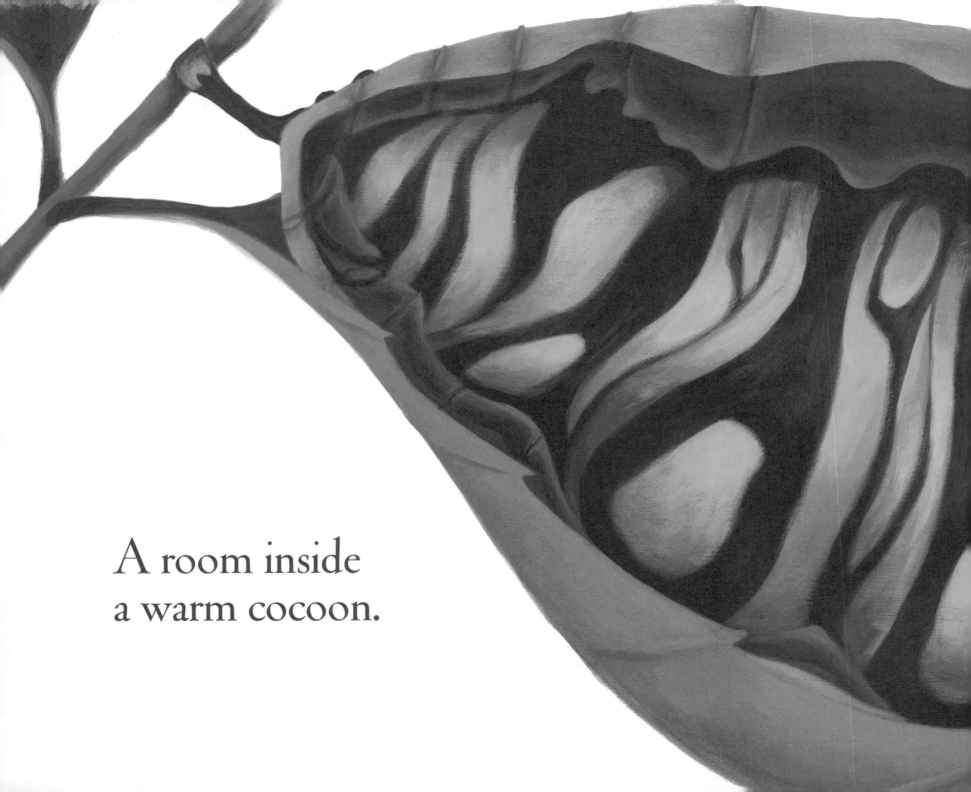

A room inside
a warm cocoon.

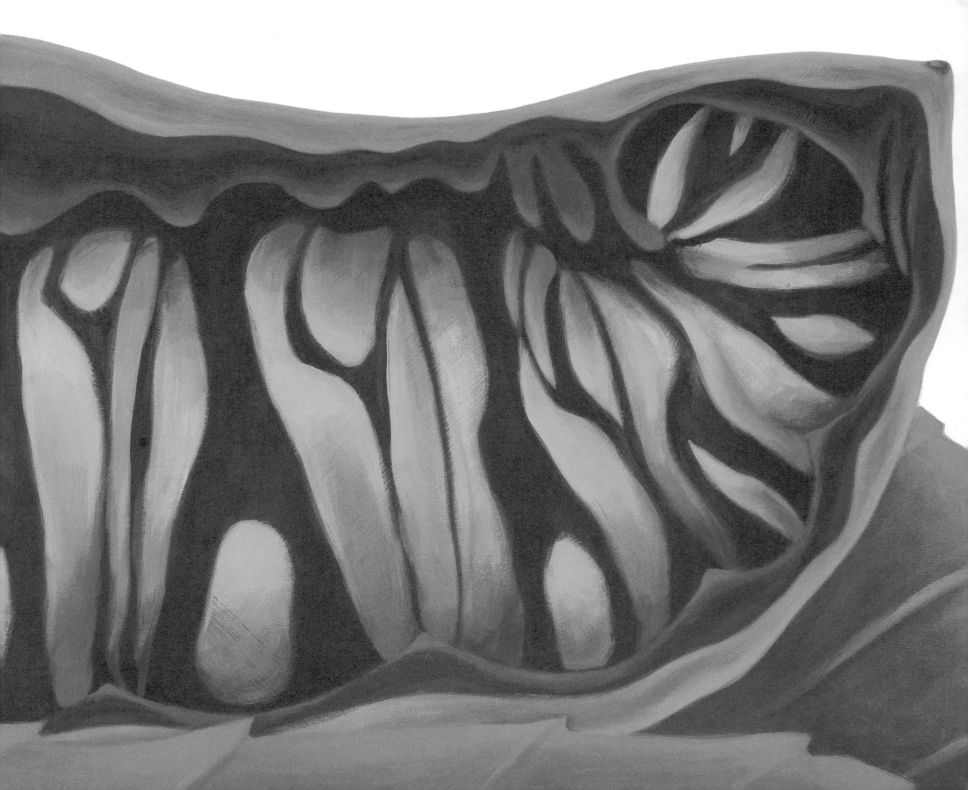

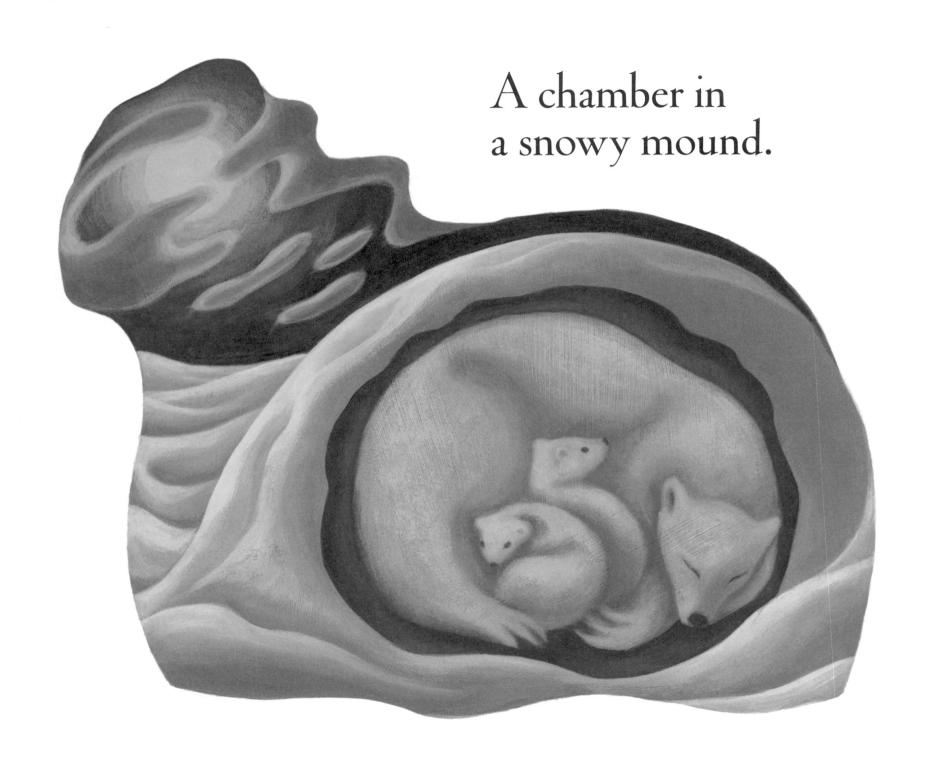

A chamber in
a snowy mound.

A busy town beneath
the ground.

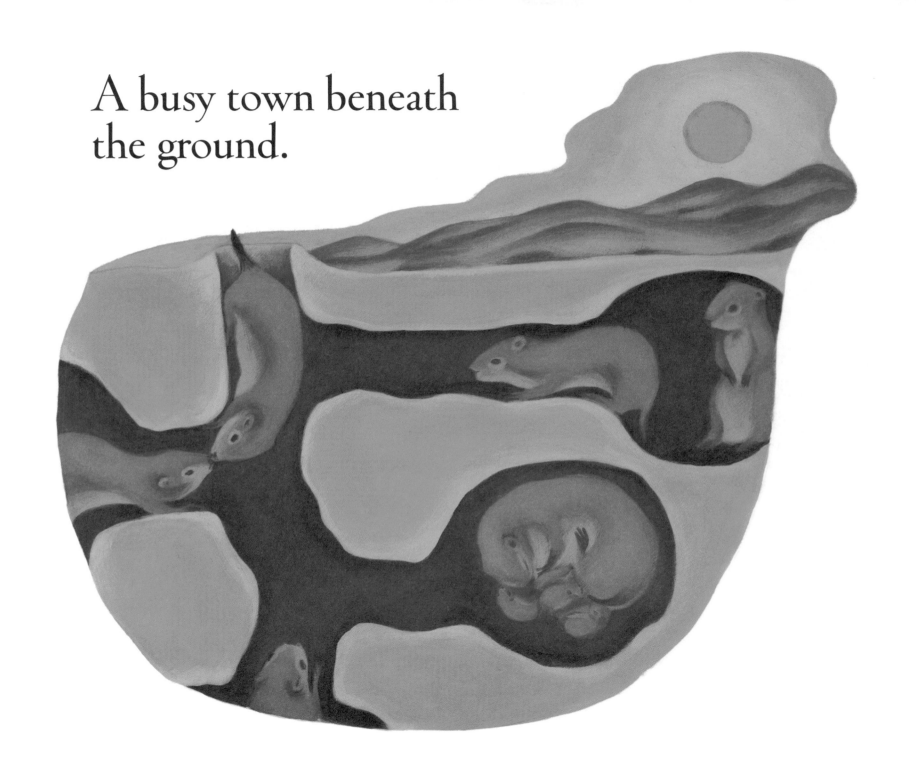

A silent cave.

A secret den.

A warren in a grassy glen.

A sloping cliff
above the shore.

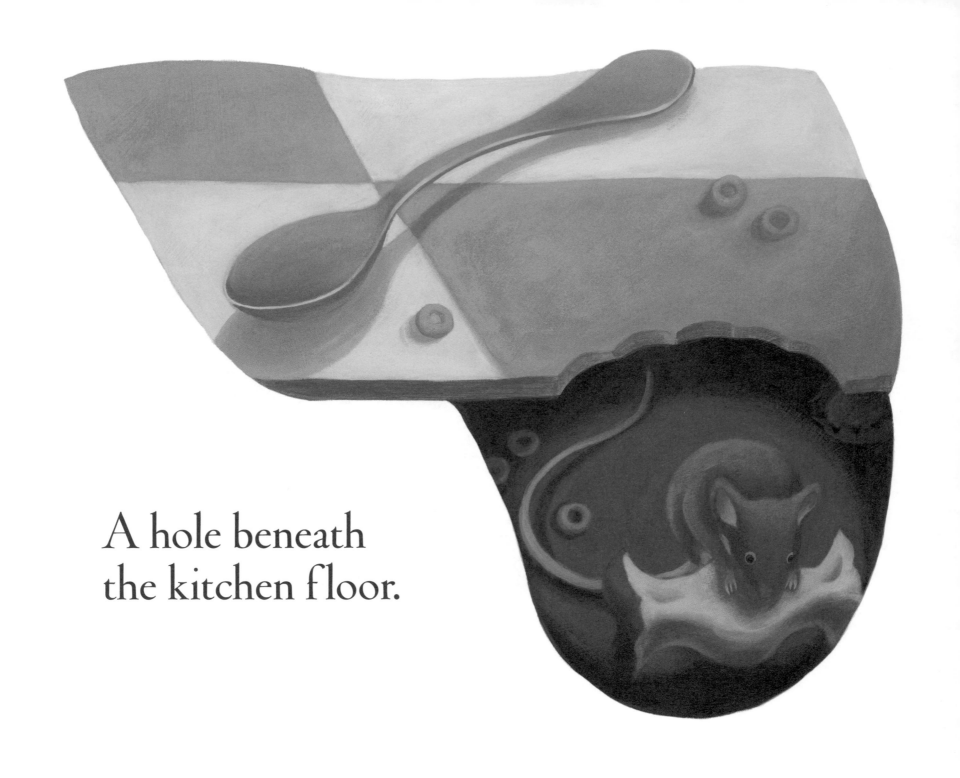

A hole beneath
the kitchen floor.

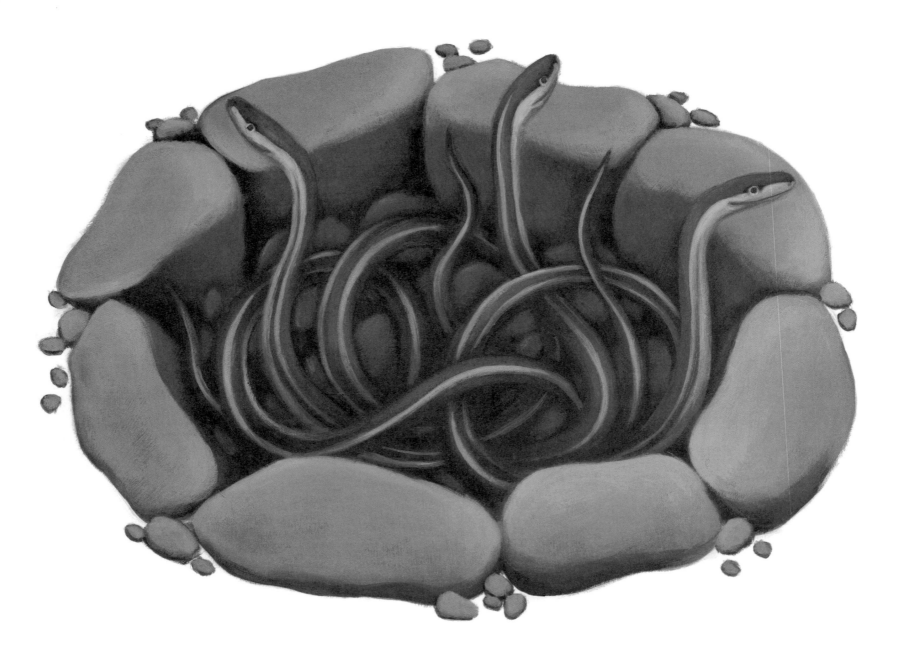

A rocky pit.

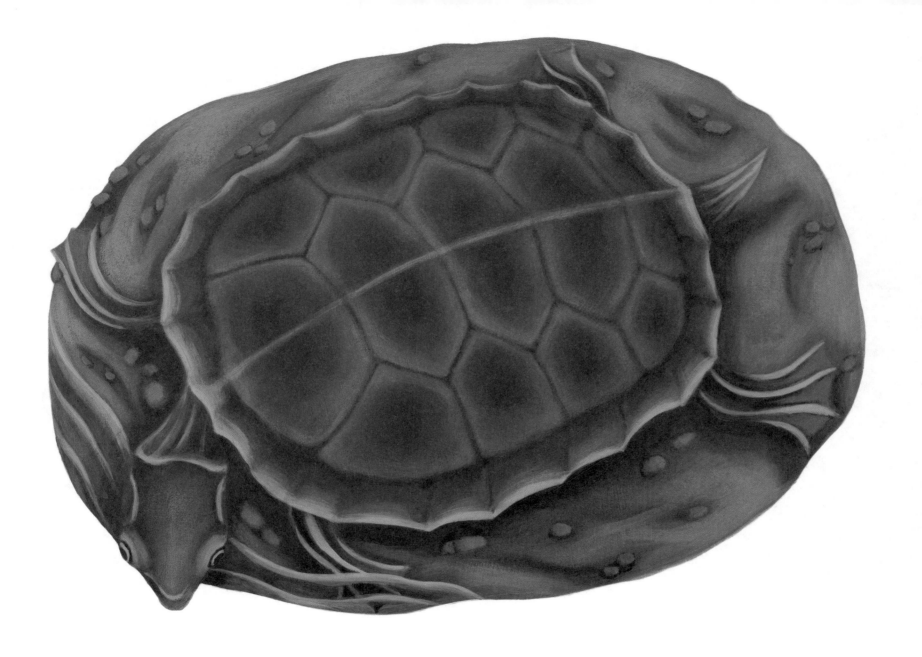

An armor case.

A shell that's carried place to place.

A hollow space
inside a tree.

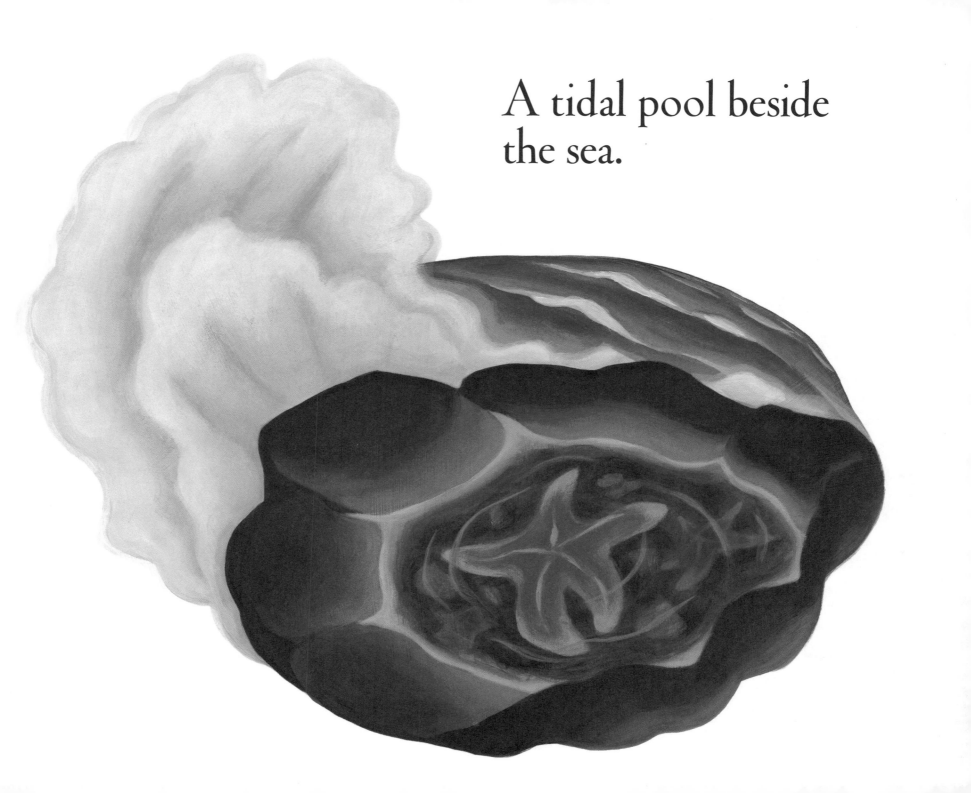

A tidal pool beside the sea.

A home's a house, a den, a nest.

A home is someplace
safe and snug.

A place to hug.

A place to share,

A place to rest.

A place to play,